Five Lectures on Reincarnation

SWAMI ABHEDANANDA

1901

TABLE OF CONTENTS

REINCARNATION

The visible phenomena of the universe are bound by the universal law of cause and effect. The effect is visible or perceptible, while the cause is invisible or imperceptible. The falling of an apple from a tree is the effect of a certain invisible force called gravitation. Although the force cannot be perceived by the senses, its expression is visible. All perceptible phenomena are but the various expressions of different forces which act as invisible agents upon the subtle and imperceptible forms of matter. These invisible agents or forces together with the imperceptible particles of matter make up the subtle states of the phenomenal universe. When a subtle force becomes objectified, it appears as a gross object. Therefore, we can say, that every gross form is an expression of some subtle force acting upon the subtle particles of matter. The minute particles of hydrogen and oxygen when combined by chemical force, appear in the gross form of water. Water can never be separated from hydrogen and oxygen, which are its subtle component parts. Its existence depends upon that of its component parts, or in other words, upon its subtle form. If the subtle state changes, the gross manifestation will also change. The peculiarity in the gross form of a plant depends upon the peculiar nature of its subtle form, the seed. The peculiar nature of the gross forms in the animal kingdom depends upon the subtle forms which manifest variously in each of the intermediate stages between the microscopic unit of living matter and the highest man. The gross human body is closely related to its subtle body. Not only this, but every movement or change in the physical form is caused by the activity and change of the subtle body. If the subtle body be affected or changed a little, the gross body will also be affected similarly. The material body being the expression of the subtle body, its birth, growth, decay and death depend upon the changes of the subtle body. As long as the subtle body remains, it will continue to express itself in a corresponding gross form.

Now let us understand clearly what we mean by a subtle body. It is nothing but a minute germ of a living substance. It contains the invisible particles of matter which are held together by vital force, and it also possesses mind or thought-force in a potential state, just as the seed of a plant contains in it the life force and the power of growth. According to Vedanta, the subtle body consists of Antahkaranam, that is, the internal organ or the mind substance with its various modifications, mind, intellect, egoism, memory, the five instruments of perception: the powers of seeing, hearing, smelling, tasting and touching; the five instruments of action, such as the powers of seizing, moving, speaking, evacuating, and generating, and the five Prânas. Prâna is a Sanskrit word which means vital energy or the life-sustaining power in us. Although Prâna is one, it takes five different names on account of the five different functions it performs. This word Prâna includes the five manifestations of the vital force: First, that power which moves the lungs and draws the atmospheric air from outside into the system. This is also called Prâna. Second, that power which throws out of the system such things as are not wanted. It is called in Sanskrit Apâna. Third, it takes the name of Samâna, as performing digestive functions and carrying the extract of food to every part of the body. It is called Udâna when it is the cause of bringing down food from the mouth through the alimentary canal to the stomach, and also when it is the cause of the power of speech. The fifth power of Prâna is that which works in every part of the nervous system from head to foot, through every canal, which keeps the shape of the body, preserves it from putrefaction, and gives health and life to every cell and organ. These are the various manifestations of the vital force or Prâna. These subtle powers together with the non-composite elements of the gross body, or the ethereal particles of subtle matter, and also with the potentialities of all the impressions, ideas and tendencies which each individual gathers in one life, make up his subtle body. As a resultant of all the different actions of mind and body which an individual performs in his present life, will be the tendencies and desires in his future life; nothing will be lost.

Every action of body or mind which we do, every thought which we think, becomes fine, and is stored up in the form of a Samskâra or impression in our minds. It remains latent for some time, and then it rises up in the form of a mental wave and produces new desires. These desires are called in Vedanta, Vâsanâs. Vâsanâs or strong desires are the manufacturers of new bodies. If Vâsanâ or longing for worldly pleasures and objects remains in anybody, even after hundreds of births, that person will be born again. Nothing can prevent the course of strong desires. Desires must be fulfilled sooner or later.

Every voluntary or involuntary action of the body, sense or mind must correspond to the dormant impressions stored up in the subtle body. Although growth, the process of nourishment and all the changes of the gross physical body take place according to the necessarily acting causes, yet the whole series of actions, and consequently every individual act, the condition of the body which accomplishes it, nay, the whole process in and through which the body exists, are nothing but the outward expressions of the latent impressions stored up in the subtle body. Upon these rests the perfect suitableness of the animal or human body to the animal or human nature of one's impressions. The organs of the senses must therefore completely correspond to the principal desires which are the strongest and most ready to manifest. They are the visible expressions of these desires. If there be no hunger or desire to eat, teeth, throat and bowels will be of no use. If there be no desire for grasping and moving, hands and legs will be useless. Similarly it can be shown that the desire for seeing, hearing, etc., has produced the eye, ear, etc. If I have no desire to use my hand, and if I do not use it at all, within a few months it will wither away and die. In India there are some religious fanatics who hold up their arms and do not use them at all; after a few months their arms wither and become stiff and dead. A person who lies on his back for six months loses the power of walking. There are many such instances which prove the injurious effects of the disuse of our limbs and organs.

As the human form, generally, corresponds to the human will, generally, so the individual bodily structure corresponds to the character, desires, will and thought of the individual. Therefore the outer nature is nothing but the expression of the inner nature. This inner nature of each individual is what re-incarnates or expresses itself successively in various forms, one after another. When a man dies the individual ego or Jîva (as it is called in Sanskrit), which means the germ of life or the living soul of man, is not destroyed, but it continues to exist in an invisible form. It remains like a permanent thread stringing together the separate lives by the law of cause and effect. The subtle body is like a water-globule which sprang in the beginningless past from the eternal ocean of Reality; and it contains the reflection of the unchangeable light of Intelligence. As a water-globule remains sometimes in an invisible vapory state in a cloud, then in rain or snow or ice, and again as steam or in mud, but is never destroyed, so the subtle body sometimes remains unmanifested and sometimes expresses itself in gross forms of animal or human beings, according to the desires and tendencies that are ready to manifest. It may go to heaven, that is, to some other planet, or it may be born again on this earth. It depends on the nature and strength of one's life-long tendency and bent of mind. This idea is clearly expressed in Vedanta. "The thought, will or desire which is extremely strong during lifetime, will become predominant at the time of death and will mould the inner nature of the dying person. The newly moulded inner nature will express in a new form." (Bhagavad Gîtâ.) The thought, will or desire which moulds the inner nature has the power of selecting or attracting such conditions or environments as will help it in its way of manifestation. This process corresponds in some respects to the law of "natural selection."

We shall be better able to understand that process by studying how the seeds of different trees select from the common environments different materials, and absorb and assimilate different quantities of elements. Suppose two seeds, one of an oak and the other of a chestnut, are planted in a pot. The power of growth in both the seeds is of the same nature. The environments, earth, water, heat and light are the same. But still there is some peculiarity in each of the seeds, which will absorb from the common environments different quantities of elements and other properties which are fit to help the growth of the peculiar nature and form of the fruit, flower, leaves of each tree. Suppose the chestnut is a horse-chestnut. If, under different conditions, the peculiar nature of the horse-chestnut changes into that of a sweet chestnut, then, along with the changes in the seed, the whole nature of the tree, leaves, fruits will also be changed. It will no more attract, absorb or assimilate those substances and qualities of the environments which it did when it was a horse-chestnut. Similarly, through the law of "natural selection" the newly moulded thought-body of the dying person will choose and attract such parts from the common environments as are helpful to its proper expression or manifestation. Parents are nothing but the principal parts of the environment of the re-incarnating individual. The newly moulded inner nature or subtle body of the individual will by the law of "natural selection" involuntarily choose, or be unconsciously drawn to, as it were, its suitable parents and will be born of them. As, for instance, if I have a strong desire to become an artist, and if after a life-long struggle I do not succeed in being the greatest, after the death of the body I will be born of such parents and with such environments as will help me to become the best artist.

The whole process is expressed in Eastern philosophy by the doctrine of the Reincarnation of the individual soul. Although this doctrine is commonly rejected in the West, it is unreservedly accepted by the vast majority of mankind of the present day, as it was in past centuries. The scientific explanation of this theory we find nowhere except in the writings of the Hindus; still we know that from very ancient times it was believed by the philosophers, sages and prophets of different countries. The ancient civilization of Egypt was built upon a crude form of the doctrine of Reincarnation. Herodotus says: "The Egyptians propounded the theory that the human soul is imperishable, and that where the body of any one dies it enters into some other creature that may be ready to receive it." Pythagoras and his disciples spread it through Greece and Italy. Pythagoras says: "All has soul; all is soul wandering in the organic world, and obeying eternal will or law."

In Dryden's Ovid we read:—

"Death has no power the immortal soul to slay,
That, when its present body turns to clay,
Seeks a fresh home, and with unlessened might
Inspires another frame with life and light."

It was the keynote of Plato's philosophy. Plato says: "Soul is older than body. Souls are continually born over again into this life." The idea of Reincarnation was spread widely in Greece and Italy by Pythagoras, Empedocles, Plato, Virgil and Ovid. It was known to the Neo-Platonists, Plotinus and Proclus. Plotinus says: "The soul leaving the body becomes that power which it has most developed. Let us fly then from here below and rise to the intellectual world, that we may not fall into a purely sensible life by allowing ourselves to follow sensible images...." It was the fundamental principle of the religion of the Persian Magi. Alexander the Great accepted this idea after coming in contact with the Hindu philosophers. Julius Caesar found that the Gauls had some belief regarding the pre-existence of the human soul. The Druids of old Gaul believed that the souls of men transmigrate into those bodies whose habits and characters they most resemble. Celts and Britons were impressed with this idea. It was a favorite theme of the Arab philosophers and many Mahomedan Sufis. The Jews adopted it after the Babylonian captivity. Philo of Alexandria, who was a contemporary of Christ, preached amongst the Hebrews the Platonic idea of the pre-existence and rebirth of human souls. Philo says: "The company of disembodied souls is distributed in various orders. The law of some of them is to enter mortal bodies, and after certain prescribed periods be again set free." John the Baptist was according to the Jews a second Elijah; Jesus was believed by many to be the re-appearance of some other prophet. (See Matt, xvi, 14, also xvii, 12.) Solomon says in his Book of Wisdom: "I was a child of good nature and a good soul came to me, or rather because I was good I came into an undefiled body."

The Talmud and Cabala teach the same thing. In the Talmud it is said that Abel's soul passed into the body of Seth, and then into that of Moses. Along with the spread of the Cabala this doctrine (which was known as Transmigration and Metempsychosis) "began to take root in Judaism and then it gained believers even among men who were little inclined towards Mysticism. Juda ben Asher (Asheri) for instance, discussing this doctrine in a letter to his father endeavored to place it upon a philosophical basis." (Jewish Encyclopedia, Vol. XII, p. 232.) We also read, "The Cabalists eagerly adopted the doctrine on account of the vast field it offered to mystic speculations. Moreover it was almost a necessary corollary of their psychological system. The absolute condition of the soul is, according to them, its return, after developing all those perfections, the germs of which are eternally implanted in it, to the Infinite Source from which it emanated. Another term of life must therefore be vouchsafed to those souls which have not fulfilled their destiny here below, and have not been sufficiently purified for the state of union with the Primordial Cause. Hence if the soul, on its first assumption of a human body and sojourn on earth, fails to acquire that experience for which it descended from heaven and becomes contaminated by that which is polluting, it must reinhabit a body till it is able to ascend in a purified state through repeated trials." This is the theory of the Zohar, which says: "All souls are subject to transmigration; and men do not know the ways of the Holy One, blessed be He! They do not know that they are brought before the tribunal both before they enter into this world and after they leave it; they are ignorant of the many transmigrations and secret probations which they have to undergo, and of the number of souls and spirits which enter into this world and which do not return to the palace of the Heavenly King. Men do not know how the souls revolve like a stone which is thrown from a sling. But the time is at hand when these mysteries will be disclosed." (Zohar, II, 99 b.)

Like many of the Church Fathers the Cabalists used as their main argument in favor of the doctrine of metempsychosis the justice of God. But for the belief in metempsychosis, they maintained, the question why God often permits the wicked to lead a happy life while many righteous are miserable would be unanswerable. Then too the infliction of pain upon children would be an act of cruelty unless it is imposed in punishment of sin committed by the soul in a previous state. Isaac Abravanel sees in the commandment of the Levirate a proof of the doctrine of metempsychosis for which he gives the following reasons: (1) God in His mercy willed that another trial should be given to the soul, which having yielded to the sanguine temperament of the body had committed a capital sin, such as murder, adultery, etc.; (2) it is only just that when a man dies young a chance should be given to his soul to execute in another body the good deeds which it had not time to perform in the first body; (3) the soul of the wicked sometimes passes into another body in order to receive its deserved punishment here below instead of in the other world where it would be much more severe. (Commentary on Deuteronomy, XXV, 5.)

Christianity is not exempt from this idea. Origen and other Church Fathers believed in it. Origen says: "For God, justly disposing of his creatures according to their desert, united the diversities of minds in one congruous world, that he might, as it were, adorn his mansion (in which ought to be not only vases of gold and silver, but of wood also and clay, and some to honor and some to dishonor) with these diverse vases, minds or souls. To these causes the world owes its diversity, while Divine Providence disposes each according to his tendency, mind and disposition." He also says: "I think this is a question how it happens that the human mind is influenced now by the good, now by the evil. The causes of this I suspect to be more ancient than this corporeal birth." The idea of Reincarnation spread so fast amongst the early Christians that Justinian was obliged to suppress it by passing a law in the Council of Constantinople in 538 A.D. The law was this: "Whoever shall support the mythical presentation of the pre-existence of the soul, and the consequently wonderful opinion of its return, let him be Anathema." The Gnostics and Manichaeans propagated the tenets of Reincarnation amongst the mediaeval sects such as the Bogomiles and Paulicians. Some of the followers of this so-called erroneous belief were cruelly persecuted in 385 A.D.

In the seventeenth century some of the Cambridge Platonists, as Dr. Henry More and others, accepted the idea of rebirth. Most of the German philosophers of the middle ages and of recent days have advocated and upheld this doctrine. Many quotations can be given from the writings of great thinkers, like Kant, Scotus, Schelling, Fichte, Leibnitz, Schopenhauer, Giardano Bruno, Goethe, Lessing, Herder and a host of others. The great skeptic Hume says in his posthumous essay on "The Immortality of the Soul," "The metempsychosis is therefore the only system of this kind that philosophy can hearken to." Scientists like Flammarion and Huxley have supported this doctrine of Reincarnation. Professor Huxley says: "None but hasty thinkers will reject it on the ground of inherent absurdity. Like the doctrine of evolution itself, that of transmigration has its roots in the world of reality." ("Evolution and Ethics," p. 61.)

Some of the theological leaders have preached it. The eminent German theologian Dr. Julius Müller supports this theory in his work on "The Christian Doctrine of Sin." Prominent theologians, such as Dr. Dorner, Ernesti, Rückert, Edward Beecher, Henry Ward Beecher, Phillips Brooks, preached many a time touching the question of the pre-existence and rebirth of the individual soul. Swedenborg and Emerson maintained it. Emerson says in his essay on Experience, "We wake and find ourselves on a stair. There are stairs below us which we seem to have ascended; there are stairs above us, many a one, which go upward and out of sight."

Almost all of the poets, ancient or modern, profess it. William Wordsworth says in "Intimations of Immortality:"—

"The soul that rises with us, our life's star,
Hath had elsewhere its setting,
And cometh from afar."

Tennyson writes in the "Two Voices;"

"Or, if through lower lives I came—
Tho' all experience past became,

Consolidate in mind and frame—
I might forget my weaker lot;
For is not our first year forgot?
The haunts of memory echo not."
Walt Whitman says in "Leaves of Grass:"
"As to you, Life, I reckon you are the leavings of many deaths,
No doubt I have died myself ten thousand times before."
Similar passages can be quoted from almost all the poets of different countries. Even amongst the aboriginal tribes of Africa, Asia, North and South America, traces of this belief in the rebirth of souls is to be found. Nearly three-fourths of the population of Asia believe in the doctrine of Reincarnation, and through it they find a satisfactory explanation of the problem of life. There is no religion which denies the continuity of the individual soul after death.

Those who do not believe in Reincarnation try to explain the world of inequalities and diversities either by the one-birth theory or by the theory of hereditary transmission. Neither of these theories, however, is sufficient to explain the inequalities that we meet with in our everyday life. Those who believe in the one-birth theory, that we have come here for the first and last time, do not understand that the acquirement of wisdom and experience is the purpose of human life; nor can they explain why children who die young should come into existence and pass away without getting the opportunity to learn anything or what purpose is served by their coming thus for a few days, remaining in utter ignorance and then passing away without gaining anything whatever. The Christian dogma, based on the one-birth theory, tells us that the child which dies soon after its birth is sure to be saved and will enjoy eternal life and everlasting happiness in heaven. The Christians who really believe in this dogma ought to pray to their heavenly Father for the death of their children immediately after their birth and ought to thank the merciful Father when the grave closes over their little forms. Thus the one-birth theory of Christian theology does not remove any difficulty.

Two great religions, Judaism with its two offspring—Christianity and Mahomedanism—and Zoroastrianism, still uphold the one-birth theory.

The followers of these, shutting their eyes to the absurdity and unreasonableness of such a theory, believe that human souls are created out of nothing at the time of the birth of their bodies and that they continue to exist throughout eternity either to suffer or to enjoy because of the deeds performed during the short period of their earthly existence. Here the question arises why should a man be held responsible throughout eternity for the works which he was forced or predestined to perform by the will of the Lord of the universe? The theory of predestination and grace, instead of explaining the difficulty, makes God partial and unjust. If the omnipotent personal God created human souls out of nothing, could He not make all souls equally good and happy? Why does He make one to enjoy all the blessings of life and another to suffer all miseries throughout eternity? Why is one born with good tendencies and another with evil ones? Why is one man virtuous throughout his life and another bestial? Why is one born intelligent and another idiotic? If God out of His own will made all these inequalities, or, in other words, if God created one man to suffer and another to enjoy, then how partial and unjust must He be! He must be worse than a tyrant. How can we worship Him, how call Him just and merciful?

Some people try to save God from this charge of partiality and injustice by saying that all good things of this universe are the work of God, and all evil things are the work of a demon or Satan. God created everything good, but it was Satan who brought evil into this world and made everything bad. Now let us see how far such a statement is logically correct. Good and evil are two relative terms; the existence of one depends upon that of the other. Good cannot exist without evil, and evil cannot exist without being related to good. When God created what we call good, He must have created evil at the same time, otherwise He could not create good alone. If the creator of evil, call him by whatever name you like, had brought evil into this world, he must have created it simultaneously with God; otherwise it would have been impossible for God to create good, which can exist only as related to evil. As such they will have to admit that the Creators of good and evil sat together at the same time to create this world, which is a mixture of good and evil. Consequently, both of them are equally powerful, and limited by each other. Therefore neither of them is infinite in powers or omnipotent. So we cannot say that the Almighty God of the universe created good alone and not the evil.

Another argument which the Vedantists advance in support of the theory of Reincarnation is that "Nothing is destroyed in the universe." Destruction in the sense of the annihilation of a thing is unknown to the Vedantic philosophers, just as it is unknown to the modern scientists. They say "non-existence can never become existence and existence can never become non-existence;" or, in other words, that which did not exist can never exist, and conversely that which exists in any form can never become non-existent. This is the law of nature. As such, the impressions or ideas which we now have, together with the powers which we possess, will not be destroyed but will remain with us in some form or other. Our bodies may change, but the powers, Karma, Samskaras or impressions and the materials which manufactured our bodies must remain in us in an unmanifested form. They will never be destroyed. Again science tells us that that which remains in an unmanifested or potential state must at some time or other be manifested in a kinetic or actual form. Therefore we shall get other bodies, sooner or later. It is for this reason said in the "Bhagavad Gîtâ": "Birth must be followed by death and death must be followed by birth." Such a continuously recurring series of births and deaths each germ of life must go through. Another consideration is that the beginning, ending and continuing are conceptions of the human mind; their significance depends entirely upon our conception of time. But we all know that time has no absolute existence. It is merely a form of our knowledge of our own existence in relation to that of nature. The conception of time vanishes at the sleep of death, just as it does every night when we are in sound sleep. Death resembles the state of our sound sleep. The soul wakes up from the sleep of death just in the same manner as the insects awake in spring after sleeping the long and rigid winter-sleep, as a chrysalis in the bed of a cocoon spun by itself in autumn. Nature teaches us the great lesson of rebirth and the similarity between sleep and death by the rejuvenation of the chrysalis in the spring. After death the soul wakes up and puts on or manufactures the garment of a new body, just in the same manner as we put on new clothes after throwing away the old and worn-out ones. Thus the soul continues to manifest itself over and over again either on the human or any other plane of existence, being bound by the Law of Karma or of Cause and Sequence.

"Death, so called, is but older matter dressed
In some new form. And in a varied vest,
From tenement to tenement though tossed,
The soul is still the same, the figure only lost."
Poem on Pythagoras, Dryden's Ovid.

Here it may be asked, if we existed before our birth why do we not remember? This is one of the strongest objections often raised against the belief in pre-existence. Some people deny the existence of the soul in the past simply because they cannot remember the events of their past. Others, again, who hold memory as the standard of existence, say, if our memory of the present ceases to exist at the time of death, with it we shall also cease to be; we cannot be immortal; because they hold that memory is the standard of life, and if we do not remember then we are not the same beings.

Vedanta answers these questions by saying that it is possible for us to remember our previous existences. Those who have read "Raja Yoga" will recall that in the 18th aphorism of the third chapter it is said: "By perceiving the Samskâras one acquires the knowledge of past lives." Here the Samskâras mean the impressions of the past experience which lie dormant in our subliminal self, and are never lost. Memory is nothing but the awakening and rising of latent impressions above the threshold of consciousness. A Raja Yogi, through powerful concentration upon these dormant impressions of the subconscious mind, can remember all the events of his past lives. There have been many instances in India of Yogis who could know not only their own past lives but correctly tell those of others. It is said that Buddha remembered five hundred of his previous births.

Our subliminal self, or the subconscious mind, is the storehouse of all the impressions that we gather through our experiences during our lifetime. They are stored up, pigeon-holed there, in the Chitta, as it is called in Vedanta. "Chitta" means the same subconscious mind or subliminal self which is the storehouse of all impressions and experiences. And these impressions remain latent until favorable conditions rouse them and bring them out on the plane of consciousness. Here let us take an illustration: In a dark room pictures are thrown on a screen by lantern-slides. The room is absolutely dark. We are looking at the pictures. Suppose we open a window and allow the rays of the midday sun to fall upon the screen. Would we be able to see those pictures? No. Why? Because the more powerful flood of light will subdue the light of the lantern and the pictures. But although they are invisible to our eyes we cannot deny their existence on the screen. Similarly, the pictures of the events of our previous lives upon the screen of the subliminal self may be invisible to us at present, but they exist there. Why are they invisible to us now? Because the more powerful light of sense-consciousness has subdued them. If we close the windows and doors of our senses from outside contact and darken the inner chamber of our self, then by focusing the light of consciousness and concentrating the mental rays we shall be able to know and remember our past lives, and all the events and experiences thereof. Those who wish therefore to develop their memory and remember their past should practice Raja Yoga and learn the method of acquiring the power of concentration by shutting the doors and windows of their senses. And that power of concentration must be helped by the power of self-control. That is, by controlling the doors and windows of our own senses.

These dormant impressions, whether we remember them or not, are the chief factors in moulding our individual characters with which we are born, and they are the causes of the inequalities and diversities which we find around us. When we study the characters and powers of geniuses and prodigies we cannot deny the pre-existence of the soul. Whatever the soul has mastered in a previous life manifests in the present. The memory of particular events is not so important. If we possess the wisdom and knowledge which we gathered in our previous lives, then it matters very little whether or not we remember the particular events, or the struggles which we went through in order to gain that knowledge. Those particular things may not come to us in our memory, but we have not lost the wisdom. Now, study your own present life and you will see that in this life you have gained some experience. The particular events and the struggles which you went through are passing out of your memory, but the experience, the knowledge which you have gained through that experience, has moulded your character, has shaped you in a different manner. You will not have to go through those different events again to remember; how you acquired that experience is not necessary; the wisdom gained is quite enough.

Then, again, we find among ourselves persons who are born with some wonderful powers. Take, for instance, the power of self-control. One is born with the power of self-control highly developed, and that self-control may not be acquired by another after years of hard struggle. Why is there this difference? Bhagavan Sri Ramakrishna was born with God-consciousness, and he went into the highest state of Samâdhi when he was four years old; but this state is very difficult for other Yogis to acquire. There was a Yogi who came to see Ramakrishna. He was an old man and possessed wonderful powers, and he said: "I have struggled for forty years to acquire that state which is natural with you." There are many such instances which show that pre-existence is a fact, and that these latent or dormant impressions of previous lives are the chief factors in moulding the individual character without depending upon the memory of the past. Because we cannot remember our past, because of the loss of memory of the particular events, the soul's progress is not arrested. The soul will continue to progress further and further, even though the memory may be weak.

Each individual soul possesses this storehouse of previous experiences in the background, in the subconscious mind. Take the instance of two lovers. What is love? It is the attraction between two souls. This love does not die with the death of the body. True love survives death and continues to grow, to become stronger and stronger. Eventually it brings the two souls together and makes them one. The theory of pre-existence alone can explain why two souls at first sight know each other and become attached to each other by the tie of friendship. This mutual love will continue to grow and will become stronger, and in the end will bring these lovers together, no matter where they go. Therefore, Vedanta does not say that the death of the body will end the attraction or the attachment of two souls; but as the souls are immortal so their relation will continue forever.

The Yogis know how to develop memory and how to read past lives. They say, time and space exist in relation to our present mental condition; if we can rise above this plane, our higher mind sees the past and future just as we see things before our eyes. Those who wish to satisfy the idle curiosity of their minds may spend their energy by trying to recollect their past lives. But I think it will be much more helpful to us if we devote our time and energy in moulding our future and in trying to be better than we are now, because the recollection of our former condition would only force us to make a bad use of the present. How unhappy he must be who knows that the wicked deeds of his past life will surely react on him and will bring distress, misery, unhappiness or suffering within a few days or a few months. Such a man would be so restless and unhappy that he would not be able to do any work properly; he would constantly think in what form misery would appear to him. He would not be able to eat or even sleep. He would be most miserable. Therefore we ought to regard it as a great blessing that we do not recollect our past lives and past deeds. Vedanta says, do not waste your valuable time in thinking of your past lives, do not look backward during the tiresome journey through the different stages of evolution, always look forward and try first to attain to the highest point of spiritual development; then if you want to know your past lives you will recollect them all. Nothing will remain unknown to you, the Knower of the universe. When the all-knowing Divine Self will manifest through you, time and space will vanish and past and future will be changed into the eternal present. Then you will say as Sri Krishna said to Arjuna, in the "Bhagavad Gita:" "Both you and I have passed through many lives; you do not recollect any, but I know them all." (Ch. iv., 5.)

HEREDITY AND REINCARNATION

Those who accept the theory of heredity deny the existence of the human soul as an entity separable from the gross physical organism. Consequently they do not discuss the question whether the individual soul existed in the past or will continue to exist after the death of the body. This kind of question does not disturb their minds. They generally maintain that the individual soul is inseparable from the body or the brain or nervous system; consequently what we call soul or the conscious entity or the thinker is produced along with the birth of the organism or brain, lasts as long as the body lasts and dies when the organism is dissolved into its elements. But those, on the other hand, who accept the theory of Reincarnation admit the existence of soul as a conscious entity which is independent of the physical organism, that it continues to live after death and that it existed before the birth of the body. The theory of heredity has always been supported by the materialistic scientists, atheists and agnostics of all ages and also by those who believe in the special creation of the first man and woman at a certain definite time and that their qualities, character, life and soul have been transmitted to all humanity through successive generations. The commonly accepted meaning of the theory of heredity is that all the well-marked peculiarities, both physical and mental, in the parents are handed on to the children; or, in other words, heredity is that property of an organism by which its peculiar nature is transmitted to its descendants.

In the whole history of humanity there has never been a time when this question of heredity has been discussed so minutely and in so many different ways as it has been in the present century. Although this theory was known in the East by the ancient Vedanta philosophers, by the Buddhists of the pre-Christian era and by the Greek philosophers in the West, still it has received a new impetus and has grown with new strength since the introduction of the Darwinian theory of the evolution of species.

Along with the latest discoveries in physiology, biology, embryology and other branches of modern science, the popular simple meaning of heredity—that the offspring not only resemble their parents among animals as well as among men, but inherit all the individual peculiarities, life and character of their parents—has taken the shape of the most complicated and difficult problem which it is almost impossible to solve. Our minds are no longer satisfied with Haeckel's definition that heredity is simply an overgrowth of the individual, a simple continuity of growth; but we want to know the particular method by which hereditary transmission takes place. We ask, how can a single cell reproduce the whole body of the offspring, its mind, character and all the peculiarities of an organism? Out of the myriads of cells of which a body is composed, what kind of cell is that which possesses the power of reproducing the peculiarities, both mental and physical, which are to be found in the form of the new-born babe? This is the most puzzling of all the problems which the scientific mind has ever encountered. The fundamental question connected with the theory of heredity is: How can a single cell of the body contain within itself all the hereditary tendencies of the hypothesis of the continuity of the germ-plasm gives an identical starting-point to each successive generation, and thus explains how it is that an identical product arises from all of them. In other words, the hypothesis explains heredity as part of the underlying problems of assimilation and of the causes which act directly during ontogeny. (Vol. I, p. 170.)

According to Weismann, all the peculiarities which we find in an organism are not inherited by the organism from that of the parents, but he says: "Nothing can arise in an organism unless the predisposition to it is pre-existent, for every acquired character is simply the reaction of the organism upon a certain stimulus." (Vol. I, p. 172.) Therefore the germ-cells do not inherit all the peculiarities of the parents, but possess the predisposition or a potentiality of the tendencies which gradually develop into individual characters.

We will be able to understand his theory better from the following quotations, which give his own words. He says: "I have called this substance 'germ-plasm,' and have assumed that it possesses a highly complex structure, conferring upon it the power of developing into a complex organism." ("Heredity," Vol. I, p. 170.) Again he says: "There is, therefore, continuity of the germ-plasm from one generation to another. One might represent the germ-plasm by the metaphor of a long, creeping rootstock from which plants arise at intervals, these latter representing the individuals of successive generations. Hence it follows that the transmission of acquired characters is an impossibility, for if the germ-plasm is not formed anew in each individual, but is derived from that which preceded it, its structure, and, above all, its molecular constitution, cannot depend upon the individual in which it happens to occur, but such an individual only forms, as it were, the nutritive soil at the expense of which the germ-plasm grows, while the latter possessed its characteristic structure from the beginning, viz., before the commencement of growth. But the tendencies of heredity, of which the germ-plasm is the bearer, depend upon this very molecular structure, and hence only those characters can be transmitted through successive generations which have been previously inherited, viz., those characters which were potentially contained in the structure of the germ-plasm. It also follows that those other characters which have been acquired by the influence of special external conditions, during the lifetime of the parent, cannot be transmitted at all." (Vol. I, p. 273.) In conclusion, Weismann writes: "But at all events we have gained this much, that the only facts which appear to directly prove a transmission of acquired characters have been refuted, and that the only firm foundation on which this hypothesis has been hitherto based has been destroyed."(Vol. I, p. 461.)

Thus we see how far the theory of heredity has been pushed by the great scientific investigators of the present age. We have no longer any right to believe in the old oft-refuted hypothesis which assumes that each individual organism produces germ-cells afresh again and again and transmits all its powers developed and acquired by the parents; but, on the contrary, we have come to know to-day that parents are nothing but mere channels through which these germ-plasms or germ-cells manifest their peculiar tendencies and powers which existed in them from the very beginning. The main point is that the germs are not created by the parents, but that they existed in previous generations.

Now, what are those germs like? Wherefrom do they acquire these tendencies, these peculiarities? That is another very difficult problem. Dr. Weismann and his followers say that these peculiarities are gained or inherited "from the common stock," but what that common stock is they do not explain. Where is that common stock and why will certain germs acquire certain tendencies and other germs retain other peculiarities? What regulates them? These questions are not solved. So far we have gathered from Dr. Weismann's explanation that the parents are not the creators of the germs but, on the contrary, that the germs existed before the birth of the body, before the growth of the body, in previous generations, or in the common stock of the universe. The previous generations are dead and gone, so we may say that they existed in the universe. We cannot now believe the old, crude, often-refuted idea that God creates the germ at the time of birth and puts into it all the powers and peculiarities of the parents. This theory makes God unjust and partial, so it does not appeal to us any more. We need better and more rational explanations. The one-birth theory, which has been preached by Christian ministers and other religionists for so many years, does not remove the difficulties, does not explain the cause of the inequalities and diversities, does not answer the question whether we acquire all the tendencies and peculiarities of the parents or whether acquired characters cannot be transmitted. We have already seen that these questions are left unsolved by the one-birth theory of Christianity and of Judaism. But this theory of "continuity of the germ-plasm" pushes the question of heredity to the door of Reincarnation. If modern science can explain what that common stock is and why and how these germs retain those peculiarities and tendencies, then the answer will be complete and not until then. The Vedanta philosophy, however, has already explained the cause of the potentiality in the germ of life or "germ-plasm" or germ-cell.

Vedanta solves this difficulty by saying that each of these germ-plasms or germ-cells is nothing but the subtle form of a reincarnating individual, containing potentially all the experiences, characters, tendencies, and desires which one had in one's previous life. It existed before the birth of the body and it will continue after the death of the body. This germ or subtle body is not the same as the astral body of the Theosophists, or the double of the metaphysical thinkers or the disembodied spirit of the Spiritualists; but it is an ethereal center of activity-physical, mental and organic. It is a center which possesses the tendency to manifest these powers on different planes of existence. It contains the minute particles of matter or ethereal substance and the life principle or vital energy by which we live and move. It also possesses the mental powers and sense powers; but all these remain latent, just as in a seed we see that the powers of growth, of assimilation and of producing flowers and fruits are latent.

At the time of death the individual soul contracts and remains in the form of a germ of life. It is for this reason, Vedanta teaches, that it is neither the will of God nor the fault of the parents that forms the characters of children, but each child is responsible for its tendencies, capacities, powers and character. It is its own "Karma" or past actions that make a child a murderer or a saint, virtuous or sinful. The stored-up potentialities in a subtle body manifest in the character of an individual.

The argument advanced by the supporters of the theory of hereditary transmission does not furnish a satisfactory explanation of the cause of the inequalities and diversities of the universe. Why is it that the children of the same parents show a marked dissimilarity to their parents and to each other?

Why do twins develop into dissimilar characters and possess opposite qualities, although they are born of the same parents at the same time and brought up under similar conditions and environments? How can heredity explain such cases? Suppose a man has five children; one is honest and saintly, another is an idiot, the third becomes a murderer, the fourth a genius or prodigy, and the fifth a cripple and diseased. Who made these dissimilarities? They cannot be accidents. There is no such thing as an accident. Every event of the universe is bound by the law of cause and effect. There must be some cause of these inequalities. Who made one honest and saintly, another an idiot, and so forth? Parents? That cannot be. They never dreamed that they would beget a murderer or a villain or an idiot. On the contrary, all parents wish their children to be the best and happiest. But in spite of such desires they get such children. Why? What is the cause? Does the theory of heredity explain it? No, not at all. Suppose a man, twenty-four years old, who has certain traits, like musical or artistic talents, such as painting and so on, has a crooked nose and other peculiarities, like cross-eyes, which resemble those of his grandfather. Suppose his grandfather died six years before he was born. Now, those who believe in the theory of heredity will say that this young man inherited all these peculiarities from his grandfather. When did he inherit? His grandfather had died six years before he was born. He inherited, of course, in the form of that germ. What is that germ like? A minute protoplasm, a jelly-like substance, and if you examine it with a powerful microscope you will hardly find any difference between it and the proto-plasmic germ of a dog, or of a cat, or of a tree. It is smaller than a pin's head. And in that state this young man inherited all these peculiarities from his grandfather; or, in other words, before he had a nose, he got a crooked nose; before he had eyes, he inherited cross-eyes, and before he had any brain, he inherited all the wonderful powers-his musical and artistic talents. Does it not seem absurd to you? Even if we admit this theory of heredity, then what do we understand? That the whole of this young man existed in the form of a protoplasm before he was born. His cross-eyes, his crooked nose, his artistic talents—all these pre-existed in the form of a protoplasmic cell. This leads up to the same thing which is taught by the theory of Reincarnation, or, in other words, if it be possible for this young man to remain in the form of a protoplasm and inherit all these things before his birth, why cannot we believe that the soul or the subtle body of this young man possessed them from the very beginning? According to Vedanta this young man was not the creature of his grandfather, but he had his own independent existence; only by coming through the channel of his parents he had received certain characteristic impressions, just as a tree in its process of growth will receive from the environments certain peculiarities when it assimilates those properties.

The doctrine of Reincarnation alone can explain satisfactorily and rationally the diversities among children and the reason of the many instances of uncommon powers and genius displayed in childhood. The theory of heredity has up to this time failed to give any good reason for them. Why is it that Pascal, when twelve years old, succeeded in discovering for himself the greater part of plane geometry. How could the shepherd Mangiamelo, when five years old, calculate like an arithmetical machine. Think of the child Zerah Colburn: when he was under eight years of age he could solve the most tremendous mathematical problems instantly and without using any figures. "In one instance he took the number 8 and raised it up progressively to the sixteenth power and instantly mentioned the result which contained 15 figures—281,474,976,710,656." Of course he was right in every figure. When asked the square root of numbers consisting of six figures, he would state the result instantly with perfect accuracy. He used to give the cube root of numbers in the hundreds of millions the very moment when it was asked. Somebody asked him once how many minutes there were in 48 years, he answered, 25,288,800.

Mozart, the great musician, wrote a sonata when he was four years old and an opera in his eighth year. Theresa Milanolla played the violin with such skill that many people thought that she must have played before her birth. There are many such instances of wonderful powers exhibited by artists and painters when they were quite young. Sankarâcharya, the great commentator of the Vedanta philosophy, finished his commentary when he was twelve years old. How can such cases be explained by the theory of hereditary transmission? Many of you have heard of the wonderful musical talents of Blind Tom. This blind negro slave was born on his master's plantation and was brought up as a typical negro. He received no training in music or in any other line. One day when his master's family were at dinner he happened to come into his master's parlor and displayed his marvelous musical power for the first time by playing on his master's piano. Afterwards he was exhibited in different states of this country. Physically he was nothing but a typical negro. His intellect was very poor, but in music he was a master. His musical talents were so great that he composed music for himself and played his own compositions. Sometimes after hearing a new piece of rapid music once, he could reproduce it note for note. Where did he get all these powers? From whom did he inherit them? His parents perhaps never heard of a piano. He never had a lesson in his life, and he could not have understood even if he had had any. Not long ago I saw a girl of about six years, who played the piano most beautifully and who could reproduce the most difficult music after hearing it once. It seems to me that she must have played the piano in her previous incarnation. This is the only explanation that we can give.

Does heredity explain such cases? No. These illustrations are sufficient to disprove the theory of "cumulative heredity". "Cumulative" means gradualness. The believers in this theory say that a genius is the result of cumulative heredity, that is, it presents itself by degrees from less genius to greater and still greater and so on. In the whole history of the genealogy of geniuses, like Homer, Plato, Shakespeare, Goethe, Raphael, there never was in their families almost Plato, almost Shakespeare, or almost Goethe. Neither is it possible to trace the extraordinary powers of any of these back

24

to any member of their ancestral line. Therefore we can say that no other theory than that of Reincarnation can explain satisfactorily the causes which produce geniuses and prodigies in this world.

Those who accept the truth of Reincarnation do not blame their parents for their poor talents, or for not possessing extraordinary powers, but they remain content with their own lot, knowing that they have made themselves as they are to-day by their own thoughts and deeds in their previous incarnations. They understand the meaning of the saying "what thou sowest thou must reap," and always endeavor to mould their future by better thoughts and better deeds. They explain all the inequalities and diversities of life and character by the law of "Karma," which governs the process of Reincarnation as well as the gradual evolution of the germs of life from lower to higher stages of existence.

EVOLUTION AND REINCARNATION

The amazing achievements of modern science have been opening every day new gates of wisdom and slowly bringing human minds nearer and nearer to the ultimate reality of the universe. The fire of knowledge kindled by science has already burnt down many dogmas and beliefs, held sacred by the superstition of the past, which stood in the way of truth-seeking minds. In the first place science has disproved the theory of the creation of the universe out of nothing by the action of some supernatural power. It has shown that the universe did not appear in its present form or come into existence all of a sudden only a few thousand years ago, but that it has taken ages to pass through different stages before it could reach its present condition. Each of these stages was directly related to a previous stage by the law of causation, which always operates in accordance with definite rules. The phenomena of the universe, according to science, are subject to evolution, or gradual change and progressive development from a relatively uniform condition to a relative complexity. From the greatest solar system down to the smallest blade of grass, everything in the universe has taken its present shape and form through this cosmic process of evolution. Our planet earth has gradually evolved, perhaps out of a nebulous mass which existed at first in a gaseous state. The sun, moon, stars, satellites and other planets have come into existence by going through innumerable changes produced by the evolutionary process of the Cosmos. Through the same process plants, insects, fishes, reptiles, birds, animals, man, and all living matter that inhabit this earth have evolved from minute germs of life into their present forms. The theory of Evolution says that man did not come into existence all of a sudden, but is related to lower animals and to plants, either directly or indirectly. The germ of life had passed through various stages of physical form before it could appear as a man. That branch of science which is called Embryology has proved the fact that "man is the epitome of the whole creation." It tells that the human body before its birth passes through all the different stages of the animal kingdom—such as the polyp, fish, reptile, dog, ape, and at last, man. If we remember that nature is always consistent, that her laws are uniform and that whatever exists in the microcosm exists also in the macrocosm, and then study nature, we shall find that all the germs of life which exist in the universe are bound to pass through stages resembling the embryonic types before they can appear in the form of man.

In explaining the theory of Evolution, science says that there are two principal factors in the process of evolution; the first is the tendency to vary, which exists in all living forms whether vegetable or animal; the second is the tendency of environment to influence that variation, either favorably or unfavorably. Without the first, evolution of any kind would be absolutely impossible. But the cause of that innate tendency to vary is still unknown to science. Upon the second depends the law of natural selection. The variation must be adapted to favorable conditions of life; consequently either the germ of life will select suitable environments or vary itself in order to suit the surrounding conditions, if they are unfavorable. But the agent of this selective process is the struggle for existence, which is a no less important factor. Thus Evolution depends on these three laws: Tendency to vary, or variation, natural selection, and struggle for existence. Science tries to explain through these three laws the physical, mental, intellectual, moral and spiritual evolution of mankind. But the theory of Evolution will remain unintelligible until science can trace the cause of that innate "tendency to vary" which exists in every stage of all living forms.

If we study closely we find that man's "self" consists of two natures, one animal and the other moral or spiritual. Animal nature includes all the animal propensities, desire for sense enjoyments, love of self, fear of death and struggle for existence. Each of these is to be found in lower animals as well as in human beings, the difference being only in degree and not in kind. In a savage tribe the expression of this animal nature is simple and natural, while in a highly civilized nation it is expressed not in a simple and straightforward manner, but in an artful and refined way. In a civilized community the same nature working through varied device, policy and plan brings the same results in a more polished form. In the struggle for existence amongst lower animals and savage tribes, those who are physically strong survive and gain advantage over those who are physically weak; while in the civilized world the same result is obtained, not by displaying physical force, but by art, diplomacy, policy, strategy and skill. Various kinds of defensive and offensive weapons have been invented to conquer those who are less skillful in using them, although they may be physically stronger. The simple expression of animal nature which we notice in savages and lower animals, by the natural process of evolution has gradually become more and more complex, as we find in the civilized nations of the world. The energy of the lower human nature is spent chiefly in the struggle for material existence.

But there is another nature in man which is higher than this. It expresses itself in various ways, but on a higher plane. Love of truth, mastery over passion, control of the senses, disinterested self-sacrifice, mercy and kindness to all creatures, desire to help the distressed, forgiveness, faith in a Supreme Being and devotion; all these are the expressions of that higher moral and spiritual nature. They cannot be explained as developed from animal nature by means of the struggle for material existence. For these qualities are not to be found in lower animals, although the struggle for existence is there. The moral and spiritual nature of human beings cannot be traced as the outgrowth or gradual development of the animal nature. There is a dispute among the Evolutionists as to the method of explaining their cause. Some say that these higher faculties have evolved out of the lower ones and have developed by variation and natural selection; while others hold that some other higher influence, law or agency is required to account for them.

Professor Huxley says: "As I have already urged, the practice of that which is ethically best—what we call goodness or virtue—involves a course of conduct which in all respects is opposed to that which leads to success in the cosmic struggle for existence. In place of ruthless self-assertion, it demands self-restraint; in place of thrusting aside or treading down all competitors, it requires that the individual shall not merely respect, but shall help his fellows; its influence is directed not so much to the survival of the fittest as to the fitting of as many as possible to survive. It repudiates the gladiatorial theory of existence. It demands that each man who enters into the enjoyment of the advantages of a polity shall be mindful of his debt to those who have laboriously constructed it, and shall take heed that no act of his weakens the fabric in which he has been permitted to live. Laws and moral precepts are directed to the end of curbing the cosmic process, and reminding the individual of his duty to the community, to the protection and influence of which he owes, if not existence itself, at least the life of something better than a brutal savage." ("Evolution and Ethics," pp. 81-82.)

Prof. Calderwood says: "So far as human organism is concerned, there seem no overwhelming obstacles to be encountered by an evolution theory, but it seems impossible under such a theory to account for the appearance of the thinking, self-regulating life distinctly human." Thus, according to some of the best thinkers, the explanation of the moral and spiritual nature of man as a development of the animal nature, is quite insufficient and unsatisfactory. The theory of natural selection in the struggle for existence cannot explain the cause of the higher nature of man. We cannot say that a theory is complete because it explains many facts. On the contrary, if it fails to explain a single fact, then it is proved to be incomplete. As such, the theory that cannot explain satisfactorily the cause of the moral and spiritual nature of man cannot be accepted as a complete theory. That explanation will be considered as complete which will explain most satisfactorily all the various manifestations of the animal, moral and spiritual nature. Moreover, supposing the "tendency to vary" has evolved into the moral and spiritual nature of man, science does not explain the cause of that tendency to vary, nor how animal nature can be transformed into moral and spiritual nature. Is that "tendency to vary" indefinite, or is it limited by any definite law? Science does not say anything about it.

The explanation of the theologians, that the spiritual nature has been superadded to the animal nature by some extra-cosmic spiritual agency is not scientific, nor does it appeal to our reason. Now let us see what Vedanta has to say on this point. Vedanta accepts evolution and admits the laws of variation and natural selection, but goes a step beyond modern science by explaining the cause of that "tendency to vary." It says, "there is nothing in the end which was not also in the beginning." It is a law which governs the process of evolution as well as the law of causation. If we admit this grand truth of nature, then it will not be difficult to explain by the theory of Evolution the gradual manifestation of the higher nature of man. The tendency of scientific monism is towards that end.

Some of the modern scientists who hold the monistic position have found out the same truth which was discovered long ago by the Vedantic philosophers in India. J. Arthur Thomson, an eminent English scientist of the present day, in his book on "The Study of Animal Life," says: "The world is one, not two-fold-, the spiritual influx is the primal reality and there is nothing in the end which was not also in the beginning." But the evolutionists do not accept this truth. Let us understand it clearly. It means that that which existed potentially at the time of the beginning of evolution has gradually manifested in the various stages and grades of evolution. If we admit that a unicellular germ of life or a bioplasm, after passing through various stages of evolution, has ultimately manifested in the form of a highly developed human being, then we shall have to admit the potentiality of all the manifested powers in that germ or bioplasm, because the law is "that which exists in the end existed also in the beginning." The animal nature, higher nature, mind, intellect, spirit, all these exist potentially in the germ of life. If we do not admit this law then the problem will arise: How can non-existence become existent? How can something come out of nothing? How can that come into existence which did not exist before? Each germ of life, according to Vedanta, possesses infinite potentialities and infinite possibilities. The powers that remain latent have the natural tendency to manifest perfectly and to become actual. In their attempt they vary according to the surrounding environments, selecting suitable conditions or remaining latent as long as circumstances do not favor them. Therefore variation, according to Vedanta, is caused by this attempt of the potential powers to become actual. When life and mind began to evolve, the possibilities of action and reaction hitherto latent in the germ of life became real and all things became, in a sense, new. Nobody can imagine the amount of latent power which a minute germ of life possesses until it expresses in gross form on the physical plane. By seeing the seed of a Banyan tree, one who has never seen the tree cannot imagine what powers lie dormant in it. When a baby is born we cannot tell whether he will be a great saint, or a wonderful artist, or a philosopher, or an idiot, or a villain of the worst type. Parents know nothing about his future. Along with his growth certain latent powers gradually begin to manifest. Those which are the strongest and most powerful will overcome others and check their course for some time; but when the powers that remain subdued by stronger ones get favorable conditions they will appear in manifested forms. As, for instance, chemical forces may slumber in matter for a thousand years, but when the contact with the re-agents sets them free, they appear again and produce certain results. For thousands of years galvanism slumbered in copper and zinc, which lay quietly beside silver. As soon as all three are brought together under the required conditions silver is consumed in flame. A dry seed of a plant may preserve the slumbering power of growth through two or three thousand years and then reappear under favorable conditions. Sir G. Wilkinson, the great archaeologist, found some grains of wheat in a hermetically sealed vase in a grave at Thebes, which must have lain there for three thousand years. When Mr. Pettigrew sowed them they grew into plants. Some vegetable roots found in the hands of an Egyptian mummy, which must have been at least two thousand years old, were planted in a flower-pot, and they grew and flourished. Thus, whenever the latent powers get favorable conditions, they manifest according to their nature, even after thousands of years.

Similarly, there are many instances of slumbering mental powers. After remaining dormant for a long period in our normal condition, they may, in certain abnormal states—such as madness, delirium, catalepsy, hypnotic sleep and so forth-flash out into luminous consciousness and throw into absolute oblivion the powers that are manifesting in the normal state. Talents for eloquence, music, painting, and uncommon ingenuity in several mechanical arts, traces of which were never found in the ordinary normal condition, are often evolved in the state of madness. Somnambulists in deep sleep have solved most difficult mathematical problems and performed various acts with results which have surprised them in their normal waking states. Thus we can understand that each individual mind is the storehouse of many powers, various impressions and ideas, some of which manifest in our normal state, while others remain latent. Our present condition of mind and body is nothing but the manifested form of certain dormant powers that exist in ourselves. If new powers are roused up and begin to manifest the whole nature will be changed into a new form. The manifestation of latent powers is at the bottom of the evolution of one species into another. This idea has been expressed in a few words by Patanjali, the great Hindu evolutionist who lived long before the Christian era. [Footnote: The reader ought to know that the doctrine of Evolution was known in India long before the Christian era. About the seventh century, B. C., Kapila, the father of Hindu Evolutionists, explained this theory for the first time through logic and science. Sir Monier Monier Williams says: "Indeed if I may be allowed the anachronism, the Hindus were Spinozites more than 2,000 years before the existence of Spinoza; and Darwinians many centuries before Darwin; and Evolutionists many centuries before the doctrine of Evolution had been accepted by the scientists of our time and before any word like Evolution existed in any language of the world." (P. 12, "Hinduism and Brahminism.") Prof. Huxley says: "To say nothing of Indian Sages to whom Evolution was a familiar notion ages before Paul of Tarsus was born." (P. 150, "Science and Hebrew Tradition.")] In the second aphorism of the fourth chapter (see "Raja Yoga," by Swami Vivekananda, p. 210) it is said, "The Evolution into another species is caused by the in-filling of nature." The nature is filled not from without but from within. Nothing is superadded to the individual soul from outside. The germs are already there, but their development depends upon their coming in contact with the necessary conditions requisite for proper manifestation. We sometimes see a wicked man suddenly become saintlike. There are instances of murderers and robbers becoming saints. A religionist will explain the cause of their sudden change, by saying that the grace of the Almighty has fallen upon them and transformed their whole nature. But Vedanta says that the moral and spiritual powers that remained latent in them have been roused up, and the result is the sudden transformation. None can tell when or how the slumbering powers will wake up and begin to manifest. The germ of life, or the individual soul as it is ordinarily called, possesses infinite possibilities. Each germ of life is studying, as it were, the book of its own nature by unfolding one page after another. When it has gone through all the pages, or, in other words, all the stages of evolution, perfect knowledge is acquired, and its course is finished. We have read our lower nature by turning each page, or, in other words, by passing through each stage of animal life from the minutest bioplasm up to the present stage of existence. Now we are studying the pages which deal with moral and spiritual laws. If any one wants to read any page over again he will do it. Just as in reading a book, if anybody feels particularly interested in any page or chapter he will read it over and over again and will not open a new page or a new chapter until he is perfectly satisfied with it. Similarly, in reading the book of life, if the individual soul likes any particular stage, he will stay there until he is perfectly satisfied with it; after that he will go forward and study other pages. One may read very slowly, and another very fast; but whether we read slowly or rapidly each one of us is bound to read the whole book of nature and attain to perfection sooner or later.

According to Vedanta, the end and aim of Evolution is the attainment of perfection. Physical evolution of animal life reached its perfection in human form. There cannot be any other form higher than human on this earth under present conditions. It is the perfection of animal form. From this we can infer that the tendency of the law of Evolution is to reach perfection. When it is attained to, the whole purpose is served. Do we see in nature any other higher form evolved out of the human body? No. Shall we not be justified if we say that the end of physical evolution is the attainment of the perfection of animal form? Again as the purpose and method of natural laws are uniform throughout the universe, the end of intellectual, moral and spiritual evolution will be attained when intellectual, moral and spiritual perfection are acquired. Intellectual perfection means perfection of intellect; and intellect is perfect when we understand the true nature of things and never mistake the unreal for the real, matter for spirit, non-eternal for eternal, or vice versa. Moral perfection consists in the destruction of selfishness; and spiritual perfection is the manifestation of the true nature of spirit which is immortal, free, divine and one with the Universal Spirit or God. Evolution attains to the highest fulfilment of its purpose when the spirit manifests perfectly. The tendency of nature is to have perfect manifestation of all her powers. When certain powers predominate they manifest first while the others remain dormant. As we find in the process of evolution, when animal nature manifests perfectly the moral and spiritual nature remain latent. Again when moral and spiritual nature manifest fully, the animal is in abeyance. It is for this reason we do not find expressions of moral and spiritual nature in lower animals or in those human beings who live like them. Man is the only animal in whom such perfect expressions of moral and spiritual nature are possible. When the individual soul begins to study its spiritual nature, its lower or animal nature is gradually eclipsed. As the higher nature becomes powerful the lower nature dwindles into insignificance; its energy is transformed into that of the higher nature, and ultimately it disappears altogether and rises no more. Then the soul becomes free from the lower or animal nature. There are many stages in the higher nature, as well as in the lower. Each of these stages binds the individual soul so long as it stays there. As it rises on a higher plane the lower stages disappear and cease to bind. But the moment that any individual, after passing through all the stages of the spiritual nature, reaches the ultimate point of perfection, he realizes his true nature which is immortal and divine. Then his true individuality manifests. For lack of true knowledge, he identified himself with each stage successively and thought that his individuality was one with the powers which were manifested in each stage. Consequently he thought by mistake that he was affected by the changes of each stage. But now he realizes that his real individuality always remained unaffected. He sees that his true individuality shines always in the same manner, although the limiting adjuncts may vary. As the light of a lamp appears of different colors, if it passes through glasses of different colors, so the light of the true individual appears as animal or human when it passes through the animal or human nature of the subtle body. The subtle body of an individual changes from animal nature through moral and spiritual into divine. As this gradual growth cannot be expected in one life we shall have to admit the truth of Reincarnation, which teaches gradual evolution of the germ of life or the individual soul through many lives and various forms. Otherwise the theory of Evolution will remain imperfect, incomplete and purposeless. The doctrine of Reincarnation differs from the accepted theory of Evolution in admitting a gradual but continuous evolution of the subtle body through many gross forms. The gross body may appear or disappear, but the subtle body continues to exist even after the dissolution of the gross body and re-manifests itself in some other form.

The theory of Reincarnation when properly understood will appear as a supplement to the theory of Evolution. Without this most important supplement the Evolution theory will never be complete and perfect. Evolution explains the process of life, while Reincarnation explains the purpose of life. Therefore, both must go hand in hand to make the explanation satisfactory in every respect.

James Freeman Clarke says: "That man has come up to his present state of development by passing through lower forms, is the popular doctrine of science to-day. What is called Evolution teaches that we have reached our present state by a very long and gradual ascent from the lowest animal organizations. It is true that the Darwinian theory takes no notice of the evolution of the soul, but only of the body. But it appears to me that a combination of the two views would remove many difficulties which still attach to the theory of natural selection and the survival of the fittest. If we are to believe in Evolution let us have the assistance of the soul itself in this development of new species. Thus science and philosophy will co-operate, nor will poetry hesitate to lend her aid." (P. 190, "Ten Great Religions," II.) Evolution of the body depends upon the evolution of the germ of life or the individual soul. When these two are combined the explanation becomes perfect.

The theory of Reincarnation is a logical necessity for the completion of the theory of Evolution. If we admit a continuous evolution of a unit of the germ of life through many gross manifestations then we unconsciously accept the teachings of the doctrine of Reincarnation. In passing through different forms and manifestations the unit of life does not lose its identity or individuality. As an atom does not lose its identity or individuality (if you allow me to suppose an atom has a kind of individuality) although it passes from the mineral, through the vegetable, into the animal, so the germ of life always preserves its identity or individuality although it passes through the different stages of evolution.

Therefore it is said in the "Bhagavad Gîtâ," as in our ordinary life the individual soul passes from a baby body to a young one and from a young to an old, and carries with it all the impressions, ideas and experience that it has gathered in its former stage of existence and reproduces them in proper time, so when a man dies the individual soul passes from an old body into a new one, and takes with it the subtle body wherein are stored up all that it experienced and gathered during its past incarnations. Knowing this, wise men are never afraid of death. They know that death is nothing but a mere change from one body into another. Therefore, if any one does not succeed in conquering the lower nature by the higher, he will try again in his next incarnation, after starting from the point which he reached in his past life. He will not begin again from the very beginning, but from the last stage at which he arrived. Thus we see that Reincarnation is the logical sequence of evolution. It completes and makes perfect that theory and explains the cause of the moral and spiritual nature of man.

WHICH IS SCIENTIFIC

RESURRECTION OR REINCARNATION?

The students of history are interested to know where the idea of resurrection first arose and how it was adopted by other nations. If we read carefully the writings ascribed to Moses and other writers of the Old Testament we find that the ancient Israelites did not believe in the Christian heaven or hell, nor in reward or punishment after death. It is doubtful whether they had any clear conception of the existence of soul after the dissolution of the human body. They had no definite idea of the hereafter. They did not believe in the resurrection either of the soul or body. Job longed for death thinking that it would end his mental agony. In Psalms we read, "Wilt Thou shew wonders to the dead? Shall the dead arise and praise Thee?" (Ps. lxxxviii, 10.) "In death there is no remembrance of Thee; in the grave who shall give Thee thanks?" (Ps. vi, 5.) Again (Ps. cxlvi, 4) it is said about princes and the son of man,—"His breath goeth forth, he returneth to his earth, in that very day his thoughts perish." "The dead praise not the Lord, neither any that go down into silence." (Ps. cxv, 17.) Solomon speaks boldly: "All things come alike to all; there is one event to the righteous and to the wicked, to the good and to the clean and to the unclean... as is the good, so is the sinner." (Eccl. ix, 2.) "Go thy way, eat thy bread with joy, and drink thy wine with a merry heart.... Live joyfully with thy wife... for there is no work, nor device, nor knowledge, nor wisdom in the grave, whither thou goest." (Eccl. ix, 7, 9, 10.) Again in verse 5 it is said: "The dead know not anything, neither have they anymore a reward, for the memory of them is forgotten." Solomon says: "For that which befalleth the sons of men befalleth beasts; even one thing befalleth them; as the one dieth, so dieth the other; yea, they have all one breath, so that a man hath no preeminence above a beast." "All go into one place; all are of the dust and all turn to dust again." "Who knoweth the spirit of man that goeth upward and the spirit of the beast that goeth downward to the earth?" (Eccl. iii, 19-21.) There are many such passages which show clearly that before the Babylonian captivity the Israelites had no belief in reward or punishment, neither in heaven nor hell nor in the resurrection of the soul. Some say that they had a belief in a sheol or pit where departed souls remained after death, but were never resurrected. But when the ancient Jews were conquered by the Persians, 536 B.C., they came in contact with a nation which had developed a belief in one God, in a heaven and a hell, in the resurrection of the dead, in reward and punishment after death, and in the last day of judgment. Under the dominion of Persia, whose rule began with the capture of Babylon and lasted from 536-333 B.C., the Jews were greatly influenced by the Persian religion. They gave up their idolatry, gradually developed social organization and had considerable liberty. About that time the Jews were divided into two classes, the Pharisees and Sadducees. Those who adopted the religious ideas of the Parsees were called Pharisees (according to some authorities the word Pharisee was the Hebrew form of Parsee), and those who followed strictly the Jewish ideas, ceremonies, rituals and beliefs were called Sadducees. The former were sharply opposed to the latter in their doctrinal beliefs. They believed in angels and spirits, they expected the resurrection of the dead and believed in future reward and punishment and also in Divine pre-ordination. The Sadducees did not step beyond the bounds of ancient Judaism. They were Orthodox and very conservative in their views. They denied the existence of angels and spirits, the resurrection of the dead, and reward and punishment after death. In Matt, xxii, 23, we read, "The same day came to him the Sadducees which say that there is no resurrection." The Sadducees were fewer in number than the Pharisees. Gradually the latter grew very powerful and after the death of Jesus their doctrines of the resurrection of the dead, and of reward and punishment after death, and the belief in angels and spirits, became the cardinal principles of the new Christian sect. Thus we see that the idea of resurrection first arose in Persia and afterwards took a prominent place in the writings of the New Testament, and since then it has been largely accepted by the Christians of the Western countries. The Zoroastrians believed that the soul of the dead hovers about the body for three nights and does not depart for the other world until the dawn after the third night. Then the righteous go to heaven and the wicked to hell. There the wicked remain until the time of renovation of the universe, that is, the judgment day. After the renovation, when Ahriman or Satan is killed, the souls of the wicked will be purified and have everlasting progress. [Footnote: "Sacred Books of the East," Vol. xvii, pp. 27, 34, 46.] The question was asked, "How shall they produce resurrection?" Ahura Mazda says: "The reply is this, that the preparation and production of the resurrection are an achievement connected with miracle, a sublimity, and afterwards also a wondrous appearance unto the creatures uninformed. The secrets and affairs of the persistent Creator are like every mystery and secret." [Footnote: Ibid., p. 80.]

The Zoroastrians believed in the resurrection, not of the physical body, but of the soul, and that it was an act of miracle. Similarly miraculous was the resurrection of Jesus. Although Jesus Himself never mentioned what kind of resurrection, whether of body or of soul that He meant and believed in, the interpretation of the writers of the Gospels shows that His disciples understood Him to mean bodily resurrection and the re-appearance of His physical form. The three days remained, just as the Zoroastrians believed. The miraculous and wondrous appearance of Jesus before His disciples was preached most vigorously by Paul. In his Epistle to the Corinthians, Paul declares emphatically that the whole of the Christian religion depends upon the miraculous resurrection and re-appearance of Jesus. Although Paul said the spiritual body of the risen dead is not the same as flesh and blood body (I Cor., XV), still that important point is generally overlooked, and the result is the belief which we find amongst some of the Christian sects; that at the call of the angels, the body will rise from the grave and the mouldering dust of bones and flesh will be put together by the miraculous power of the Almighty God. Paul says: "But now is Christ risen from the dead, and become the first fruits of them that slept" (I Cor., XV, 20). He preached that Christ was the first born from the dead, that those who believe in Christ would rise as He did and that those who would not believe in Him or in His resurrection should not rise.

We have already noticed that the Parsees believed in a miraculous resurrection; that the same miracle became more definite in the case of Jesus; and that the Christian faith was afterwards founded upon that miraculous event. Both the Parsees and the followers of Christ did not mean by resurrection any universal law, but a miracle done by certain supernatural powers. They did not give any scientific reasons for such a miracle.

But modern science denies miracles. It teaches that this universe is guided, not by miracles as the old thinkers used to believe, but by definite laws which are always consistent and universal. There cannot be any exception to those laws which are uniform throughout. If resurrection be one of those laws, then it must have existed before the birth of Jesus; as such, how could He be the first born from the dead, as described by Paul. Conversely, if Jesus was the first who rose from the dead, then resurrection cannot be a universal law. Scientists would not believe in anything which is not based upon universal laws. Some of the agnostics and materialists have gone so far as to say that Jesus did not die on the cross, but his animation was suspended when his body was taken down from the cross by Joseph of Arimathsea. When Joseph went to Pilate and craved the body of Jesus, Pilate marvelled if He were dead (Mark XV, 44), because it was only six hours after the crucifixion. Some of the modern physiologists are of opinion that temperate and strong men might live for several days on the cross. These heretical agnostics and skeptical scientists say that the body of Jesus revived after a few hours in the cool, rock-cut tomb, that he walked out of the tomb, went to Galilee and appeared before his disciples. [Footnote: Vide "Science and Christian Tradition," by Prof. Huxley, pp. 279-280.] Whatever the facts may be (nobody can now tell exactly what actually happened), it is clear that the scientists are not ready to take anything upon authority. They do not care to believe in anything because it is written in this book or that. They must have convincing proofs and a rational explanation of every phenomenon of nature. They want to penetrate into miracles in order to discover the universal laws that govern them. If they do not find any such laws, they will surely reject every event that is supposed to be caused by miraculous or supernatural powers.

The theory of a miraculous resurrection is attended with the belief that the individual soul does not exist before birth. The supporters of this theory hold that at the time of birth, the individual, being created out of nothing, comes fresh into existence. But science tells us that sudden creation out of nothing and a total destruction of anything are both impossible. Matter and force are indestructible. Science teaches evolution and not creation, and denies the intervention of any supernatural being as the cause of phenomenal changes. The theory of Resurrection ignores all these ultimate conclusions of modern science. On the contrary, the doctrine of Reincarnation, after accepting all the truths and laws of nature that have been discovered by modern science, carries them to their proper logical conclusions. Reincarnation is based upon evolution. It means a continuous evolution of an individual germ of life, and a gradual re-manifestation of all the powers and forces that exist in it potentially. Moreover, the doctrine of Reincarnation is founded on the law of cause and effect. It teaches that the cause is not outside of the effect, but lies in the effect. The cause is the potential or unmanifested state of the effect, and effect is the actual or manifested cause. There is one current of infinite force or power constantly flowing in the ocean of reality of the universe, and appearing in the innumerable forms of waves. We call one set of waves the cause of another set, but in fact that which is the cause is the potentiality of the future effect and the actuality of a previous potential cause. The underlying current is one and the same throughout. Reincarnation denies the idea that the soul has come into existence all of a sudden or has been created for the first time, but it holds that it has been existing from the beginningless past, and will exist all through eternity. The individual soul enjoys or suffers according to the acts it performs. All enjoyment and suffering are but the reactions of our actions. Actions are the causes and the reactions are the results. Our present life is the result of our past actions, and our future will be the result of the present. The actions which we are now doing will not be lost. Do you think that the thought-forces of one life-time will end suddenly after death? No. They will be conserved and remain potentially in the center and re-manifest under suitable conditions. Each human soul is nothing but a center of thought-force. This center is called in Sanskrit Sûkshma Sarîra or the subtle body of an individual. The subtle germ of life or, in other words, the invisible center of thought-forces, will manufacture a physical vehicle for expressing the latent powers that are ready for manifestation. This process will continue until the germ can express most perfectly all the powers that are coiled up in its invisible form. As the doctrine of Reincarnation is in agreement with all the physical laws, so it is based upon psychical, moral and ethical laws. As on the objective plane the law of action and reaction governs the objective phenomena, so on the subjective plane of consciousness, if the mental action or thought be good, the reaction will be good, and the reaction will be evil if the mental action be evil, because every action produces a similar reaction, A good reaction is one which makes us happy and brings pleasant sensations or peace of mind, while an evil reaction brings suffering, unpleasant sensations, and makes one miserable. Thus Reincarnation makes us free agents for action, as well as for reaping the results or reactions of those actions. In fact, we mould our own nature, according to our desires, tendencies and works.

The theory of Resurrection, as commonly understood, does not explain why one man is born with a sinful nature and another with a virtuous one. It contents itself with saying as Luther said: "Man is a beast of burden who only moves as his rider orders; sometimes God rides him and sometimes Satan." But why God should allow Satan to ride His own creature nobody can tell. At any rate, man must suffer eternally for the crimes which he is forced by Satan to commit. Moreover this theory pre-supposes predestination and that the individual soul is fore-doomed to go either to heaven or to hell. St. Augustine first started this doctrine of Predestination and Grace to explain why one is born sinful and another sinless. According to this theory, God, the merciful, favors somebody with His grace at the time of his birth and then he comes into this world ready to be saved, but the mass of humanity is born sinful and destined for eternal damnation. Very few indeed receive the gift of grace and are predestined to be saved. Moreover, this doctrine tells us that God creates man out of nothing, forbids him something, but at the same time He does not give him the power to obey His commands. Ultimately God punishes him with eternal torture on account of his weakness. The body and soul will not be separated. He will not be set free from his body, because, if it be so, there will be the end of his suffering, which God does not like. All these sufferings and punishments are predestined before his birth. Thus, St. Augustine's dogma of Predestination and Grace instead of explaining the difficulty satisfactorily brings horror and dread to human minds, while the doctrine of Reincarnation teaches gradual progress from lower to higher, through ages until the individual reaches perfection. It holds that each individual will become perfect like Jesus or Buddha or like the Father in heaven and manifest divinity either in this life or in some other. One span of life is too short for developing one's powers to perfection. If you should try to train an idiot to become a great artist or a philosopher, would you ever succeed in your attempt to make him so during his lifetime? No. And will you punish him because he cannot become so? Can a man who possesses the slightest common sense be so unreasonable? Similarly what would you think if God punishes a man because he cannot become perfect within a lifetime? It is a poor argument to say that God has given us free-will to choose between right and wrong, and we are responsible for our choice; if we choose wrongly we must be punished. The advocates of such an argument forget that at the same time God has let loose His powerful Satan to corrupt His creatures.

It reminds me of an old story. Once on a time at a certain place a prisoner was released and set free through the kindness of a tyrant. The tyrant said to the prisoner "Look here, wicked man, I give you freedom, you can go to any place; but there is one condition; if you are attacked by any wild animal you will be put in the dungeon and there will be no end to your torture." So saying he gave him freedom, but at the same time ordered his servants to let loose a hungry wolf to chase the man. You can imagine what became of the prisoner. Can we call this an act of mercy!

The doctrine of Reincarnation says that each individual soul is potentially perfect and is gradually unfolding its powers and making them actual through the process of Evolution. At every step of that process it is gaining different experiences which last only for a time. Therefore neither God nor Satan is responsible for our good or evil actions. Good and evil are like the up and down or the crest and hollow of a wave in the sea. A wave cannot rise without making a hollow somewhere in the sea. So in the infinite ocean of reality innumerable waves are constantly rising. The summit of each wave is called good, while the hollow beside it is evil or misery and the current of each individual life is constantly flowing towards the ultimate destination which we call perfection. Who can tell how long it will take to reach that goal? If anybody can attain to perfection in this life, he is no longer bound to reincarnate. If he fails he will continue to progress by taking some other body. Reincarnation does not teach, as many people think, that in the next incarnation one will begin from the very beginning, but it says that one will start from that point which one reaches before death and will keep the thread of progress unbroken. It does not teach that we go back to animal bodies after death, but that we get our bodies according to our desires, tendencies and powers. If any person has no desire to come back to this world or to any other and does not want to enjoy any particular object of pleasure, and if he is perfectly free from selfishness that person will not have to come back. The theory of Reincarnation is logical and satisfactory. While the theory of Resurrection is neither based on scientific truths nor can it logically explain the cause of life and death, Reincarnation solves all the problems of life and explains scientifically all the questions and doubts that arise in the human mind.

"Reincarnation is not easily understood by a thoughtless child deluded by the delusion of wealth, name or fame. Everything ends with death, he thinks, and thus falls again and again under the sway of death."

THEORY OF TRANSMIGRATION

The theory of transmigration is one of the oldest theories accepted by the people of the Orient to solve the problems concerning life and death as well as to explain the continuity of existence after death. This theory presupposes the existence of the soul as an entity which can live even when the gross material body is dead or dissolved into its elements. Those who deny the existence of the soul, of the self-conscious thinker and actor, as an entity distinct from the gross material body, necessarily deny this theory of transmigration. The materialistic thinkers of all ages have refused to accept this theory, because they do not admit the existence of a soul or a self-conscious thinker and actor as an entity, separate from the gross material body. Consequently they do not ask or discuss whether the soul will exist after death or not, whether it will continue to live or not. Such materialists are not the creatures of the twentieth century, but they have lived in all ages, in all countries. In India and in other civilized countries of ancient times you will find that materialistic thinkers prevailed and they gave the same arguments which we hear now from the agnostics and scientists of to-day. Their arguments are generally one-sided and unsatisfactory. They try to deduce the soul or self-conscious entity from the combination of matter or material forces, but they have not succeeded in giving a scientific proof of it. No arguments in favor of the existence of a soul as an entity will convince them, because they deny the existence of anything that cannot be perceived by sense powers. If we could bring the soul down on the sense plane and make it visible to these materialistic thinkers, and if they could make experiments upon it, then perhaps they would be convinced to a certain extent, but not until then. But how can we bring the soul down on the sense plane when it is ethereal and finer than anything that we can perceive with our senses?

Those who try to explain the cause of our earthly life by the theory of heredity do not believe in the truth of transmigration. The modern scientists, agnostics and materialists generally accept the theory of heredity and endeavor to explain everything by it; but if we examine their arguments for the theory of heredity, we shall find that the theory of transmigration is much more satisfactory, much more rational than that of heredity.

Among the followers of the great religions of the world, the majority of Christians, Jews, Mohammedans and Parsees deny the truth of transmigration. Of course, there was a time when the Christians believed in this transmigration theory. Origen and other Church Fathers accepted it until the time of Justinian, who anathematized all those who believed in Reincarnation or the pre-existence of the soul. Among the Jews we find that in the Cabala this idea of transmigration plays the most important part. In fact the Cabalists accepted this theory to explain all the difficulties that could not be explained by any other theory. But those Jews, Christians, Mohammedans and Parsees who do not believe in the theory of transmigration accept the one-birth theory; that is, that God creates the souls at the time of birth out of nothing, and these souls, having come into existence out of nothing, continue to live forever; that this is our first and last birth that we receive; we did not exist before, we are suddenly created by God, and after death each one of us will continue to live either in heaven or hell to enjoy or to suffer throughout eternity. Among the modern Spiritualists we find that those who are born and brought up with this idea of one birth do not accept the theory of transmigration. Still there are millions and millions of people all over the world who do believe in transmigration and who have found comfort and consolation in their lives as well as a satisfactory solution of the problems of life and death.

The theory of Transmigration, or Metempsychosis, as it has been called by many philosophers, originally meant the passing of a soul from one body after death into another; or, in other words, it meant that the soul after dwelling in one particular body for a certain length of time leaves it at the time of death, and in order to gain experience enters into some other body, either human, animal or angelic, which is ready to receive it. It may migrate from the human body to an angelic body and then come down on the human plane, or to the animal plane and be born again as an animal. So the original meaning of transmigration or metempsychosis was the revolution of the soul from body to body whether animal, human, angelic or of the gods. The migrating substance being a fixed quantity, with fixed qualities, chooses its form according to its taste, desire and bent of character. This idea prevailed among the ancient Egyptians, according to whom the soul, after leaving the dead body, would travel from one body to another for thousands and thousands of years in order to gain experiences in each of the different stages of life.

Among the Greek philosophers we find that Pythagoras, Plato and their followers believed in this theory of Metempsychosis or Transmigration of souls. Pythagoras says: "After death the rational mind, having been freed from the chains of the body, assumes an ethereal vehicle and passes into the region of the dead where it remains till it is sent back to this world to inhabit some other body human or animal. After undergoing successive purgations, when it is sufficiently purified, it is received among the gods and returns to the eternal source from which it first proceeded." Plato also believed in this theory. Of course we cannot tell exactly from whence Pythagoras and Plato got these ideas. Some say that they learned these doctrines from Egypt; others believed that, either directly or indirectly, they learned the theory of transmigration from India. Plato describes in "Phaedrus," in mythological language, why and how the souls take their birth upon this plane, either as human or animal. He says: "In the heaven Zeus, the Father and Lord of all creatures, drives his winged car, ordering all things and superintending them. A host of deities and spirits follow him, each fulfilling his own function. Whoever will and can follows them. After taking this round, they advance by a steep course along the inner circumference of the heavenly vault and proceed to a banquet. The chariots of the gods, being well balanced and well driven, advance easily; others with difficulty; for the vicious horse, unless the charioteer has thoroughly broken him, weighs down the car by his proclivity towards the earth, whereupon the soul is put to the extremity of toil and effort. The souls of gods reach the summit, go outside and stand upon the surface of heaven, and enjoy celestial bliss. Such is the life of the gods; other souls which follow God best and are likest to Him succeed in seeing the vision of truth and in entering into the outer world with great difficulty. The rest of the souls longing after the upper world all follow; but not being strong enough, they are carried round in the deep below, plunging, treading on one another, striving to be first, and there, in confusion and extremity of effort, many of them are lamed and have their wings broken. Thus when the soul is unable to follow and fails to behold the vision of Truth, sinks beneath the double load of forgetfulness and vice, her feathers fall from her and she drops to earth and is born again and again as human beings or as animals." Plato says: "Ten thousand years must elapse before the soul can return to the place from whence she came, for she cannot grow her wings in less." "At the end of the first thousand years, the souls of the good and of the evil kind come together to draw lots, and choose their bodies according to their tendencies and the bent of their characters. They may take any they like. Instead of receiving the natural consequences of their deeds and misdeeds of their previous lives they are allowed to choose their own lot, according to their experience and bent of character. Some, being disgusted with mankind, prefer to be born as animals, such as lions and eagles or some other animals. Others delight in trying their luck as human beings." From this mythological description we gather what Plato meant by transmigration.

This Platonic idea of transmigration or of successive lives of those who inhabit this earth has been criticized by various thinkers of modern times; and referring to this idea the late Doctor Myers, of the Psychical Research Society of London, writes in his second volume of "Human Personality": "The simple fact that such was probably the opinion of both Plato and Virgil shows that there is nothing here which is alien to the best reason or to the highest instincts of men. Nor, indeed, is it easy to realize any theory of the direct creation of spirits at such different stages of advancement as those which enter upon the earth in the guise of mortal man. There must, one feels, be some kind of continuity—some form of spiritual past." (P. 134.) Why does He not create all souls equal? Why will one soul be highly advanced spiritually while another is entirely ignorant and idiotic? This question cannot be answered, this problem cannot be solved by the special creation theory, and therefore Doctor Myers says that there is no doubt that there was some previous continuity or spiritual past of each individual soul, and therefore he tacitly admits the theory of Transmigration. Although from a scientific viewpoint he could not give any direct proof regarding this idea of a pre-existence of the soul, still he could not deny it entirely when he said: "The shaping forces which have made our bodies and our minds what they are may always have been psychical forces—from the first living slime-speck to the complex intelligences of to-day." "The old transmigrationist's view would thus possess a share of truth and the actual man would be the resultant not only of intermingling heredities on father's and mother's sides, but of intermingling heredities, one of planetary and one of cosmic scope." ("Human Personality," Vol. II, p. 267.)

But this theory of Transmigration, as described by Plato, is a little different from a similar theory which existed in India before his time. In the Platonic idea of transmigration, as we have already seen, the souls were allowed to choose their own lot according to their experience or bent of character, but not to receive the natural consequence of their deeds and misdeeds. Plato did not say anything about the law which governs souls; but in ancient India the great thinkers and philosophers explained that each individual soul is bound by the inexorable law of nature to receive its body as a natural consequence of its former deeds and misdeeds, and not to have free choice of its lot according to its bent of character. The great thinkers and philosophers of ancient India discovered the universal law of cause and effect, of action and reaction, and called it by the Sanskrit term "Karma," which means the law of cause and sequence; that every cause must be followed by an effect of a similar nature, that every action must produce similar reaction, and conversely every reaction or effect is the result of an action or cause of a similar character. Thus there is always a balance and harmony between cause and effect, between action and reaction. This law of Karma has now become a fundamental verity of modern science. It is called by different names: the scientists call it the law of causation, the law of compensation, the law of retribution, the law of action and reaction, but they all refer to the same idea,—that every cause must produce a similar result and every action must produce a similar reaction.

Now these ancient thinkers of India applied this law of Karma to explain the destiny of human souls, and it was upon this law they based the theory of Transmigration. They maintained that human souls are bound by this irresistible law and cannot get out of it; their thoughts and deeds are the causes which produce results of similar nature. So their future birth does not depend upon their whimsical, free choice, but it is limited by the thoughts and deeds or misdeeds of their previous lives. In the Platonic idea we find that the souls go according to their choice. They may not take a human form if they prefer an animal form, but in the Hindu idea of transmigration we find that it is not a result of free choice, but, if our thoughts and deeds force us to take a particular form, then we are subject to the law of Karma, which governs our future birth and the evolution of our souls. Consequently the Hindu theory of Transmigration differs fundamentally from the Platonic as well as from the Egyptian idea of Transmigration. In the Platonic and Egyptian theories we see that the souls, after leaving the body, enter into another body which is waiting to receive the migrating soul, but in the Hindu theory of Transmigration the body is not waiting to receive the migrating soul, but on the contrary the soul, being subject to the laws of evolution, manufactures the gross material body according to its desires and tendencies. Just as a germ of life will develop a grosser form by cellular subdivision, by growth, and by assimilation of the environmental conditions, so the germ of the human soul will manufacture the body by obeying the laws which govern the physical plane. Parents are nothing but the channels through which the migrating souls receive their material forms. Parents do not create the souls; they have no power to create. They can only give the suitable environments necessary for manufacturing a gross physical body. The souls come with their tendencies, with their desires, and they remain as germs of life.

Now these germs of life contain vital forces, sense powers, psychic powers, and ethereal particles of matter. At the time of death the soul contracts and withdraws all its powers from the sense organs to its innermost center, and in that contracted state it leaves the body. But these powers do not leave the soul. By the law of persistence of force and conservation of energy they remain latent in that center until environmental conditions become favorable for their remanifestation. Rebirth means the manifestation of the latent powers which exist in the germ of life or in the individual soul. These germs of life are called by different names. Leibnitz called them monads and modern scientists call them bioplasms or some such name, but the Vedanta philosophers describe them as subtle bodies. These germs or subtle bodies are subject to evolution and growth; they arise from lower to higher stages of development, from the mineral through the vegetable to the animal kingdom and eventually they become human beings and then they go on progressing.

In the Platonic theory the idea of progress, growth or gradual evolution of the soul from the lower to higher stages of existence is entirely excluded, because, as I have already said, the migrating substance is of a fixed quantity with fixed qualities, that is, these qualities do not change and are not affected by either growth or evolution. They are constant quantities. In order to differentiate these two ideas we should call the Hindu theory of Transmigration by the term "Reincarnation." The Hindu or Vedantic theory of Reincarnation, however, is not the same as the Buddhistic theory of Rebirth, for the Buddhists do not believe in the permanence of the soul entity. There is another point where the Reincarnation theory differs from Platonic transmigration. According to this theory of Reincarnation there is growth and evolution of each individual soul from the lower to higher stages of development. The soul or germ of life, after passing through the lower stages, comes to the human plane and gains experience and knowledge; and after coming to the human plane, it does not retrograde to animal bodies. The Platonic theory teaches that human souls migrate into animal bodies or angelic bodies and return from the angelic to the human or the animal, and that some of them prefer to become animals; while the theory of Reincarnation, taking its stand upon the scientific truth of gradual evolution, teaches that the human souls have already passed through different grades of the animal, nay, of the vegetable kingdom, by the natural process of evolution. After having once received the human organism, why should a soul choose to go back to the lesser and more imperfect organism of an animal? How is it possible for a lesser manifestation to hold a greater one? Why should a greater manifestation choose more limited forms in preference to those of others? This question arises in the Platonic theory of Transmigration. Therefore, the Reincarnation theory, or the theory of Transmigration according to the Hindus, rejects this idea of the going back of human souls to animal forms. We have already passed in the evolutionary process through the lower grade of animal organisms. Now that we have outgrown them why should we go back to them?

It is true, however, that in India there are many uneducated people among the Hindus who believe that human souls do migrate into animal bodies after death to gain experience and reap the results of their wicked deeds, being bound by the law of Karma; but in the Platonic theory the law of Karma plays no part in the transmigration of souls. The educated and thoughtful minds of India, however, accept the more rational and scientific theory of Reincarnation. Although there are passages in the scriptural writings of the Hindus which apparently refer to the retrogression of the human soul into animal nature, still such passages do not necessarily mean that the souls will be obliged to take animal bodies. They may live like animals even when they have human bodies, as we may find among us many people like cats and dogs and snakes in human form and they are often more vicious than natural cats, dogs or snakes. They are reaping their own Karma and manifesting their animal nature, though physically they look like human beings. This kind of retrogression is possible for one who after reaching the human plane goes backward on account of wicked thoughts and deeds on the animal plane. Such a temporary retrogression brings knowledge and helps it in its onward progress toward the manifestation of higher powers on the higher plane of consciousness. All the wicked thoughts and wicked deeds are nothing but the results of our own mistakes. What is sin? Sin is nothing but a mistake and it proceeds from ignorance. For instance, if I do not know that fire burns, I may put my finger into it and get burned. The result of this mistake is the burning of the finger and this has taught me once for all that fire burns; I shall never again put my finger into fire. So every mistake is a great teacher in the long run. No one is born so high and perfect as not to commit any mistake or any sin. Every mistake like this opens our eyes to the laws of the universe by bringing to us such results as we do not desire. As one life is not enough to gain experience in all the stages of evolution, we must have to admit the doctrine of the Reincarnation of the soul for the fulfillment of the ultimate purpose of earthly life. Professor Huxley says: "None but hasty thinkers will reject it on the ground of inherent absurdity. Like the doctrine of evolution itself that of transmigration has its roots in the world of reality."